Mysticism and the Plurality of Meaning

The Institute of Ismaili Studies
Occasional Papers —2

Mysticism and the Plurality of Meaning

The Case of the Ismailis of Rural Iran

RAFIQUE KESHAVJEE

I.B. Tauris
LONDON • NEW YORK
in association with
The Institute of Ismaili Studies
LONDON

Published in 1998 by
I.B.Tauris & Co Ltd
Victoria House
Bloomsbury Square
London WC1B 4DZ

175 Fifth Avenue
New York NY 10010

in association with
The Institute of Ismaili Studies
42–44 Grosvenor Gardens
London SW1W 0EB

In the United States of America
and in Canada distributed by
St Martin's Press
175 Fifth Avenue
New York NY 10010

A full CIP record for this book is available from the British Library
A full CIP record for this book is available from the Library of
Congress

ISBN 1 86064 231 4

Library of Congress catalog card number: available

Typeset in ITC New Baskerville by Hepton Books, Oxford
Printed and bound in Great Britain by WBC Ltd, Bridgend

The Institute of Ismaili Studies

The Institute of Ismaili Studies was established in 1977 with the object of promoting scholarship and learning on Islam, in the historical as well as contemporary contexts, and a better understanding of its relationship with other societies and faiths.

The Institute's programmes encourage a perspective which is not confined to the theological and religious heritage of Islam, but seek to explore the relationship of religious ideas to broader dimensions of society and culture. They thus encourage an interdisciplinary approach to the materials of Islamic history and thought. Particular attention is also given to issues of modernity that arise as Muslims seek to relate their heritage to the contemporary situation.

Within the Islamic tradition, the Institute's programmes seek to promote research on those areas which have, to date, received relatively little attention from scholars. These include the intellectual and literary expressions of Shi'ism in general, and Ismailism in particular.

In the context of Islamic societies, the Institute's programmes are informed by the full range and diversity of cultures in which Islam is practised today, from the Middle East, Southern and Central Asia and Africa to the industrialized societies of the West, thus taking into consideration the variety of contexts which shape the ideals, beliefs and practices of the faith.

The publications of the Institute fall into several distinct categories:

1. Occasional papers or essays addressing broad themes of the

relationship between religion and society in the historical as well as modern contexts, with special reference to Islam, but encompassing, where appropriate, other faiths and cultures.
2. Proceedings of conferences or symposia.
3. Works exploring a specific theme or aspect of Islamic faith or culture, or the contribution of an individual figure or writer.
4. Translations of poetic or literary texts.
5. Editions or translations of significant texts of a primary or secondary nature.
6. Ismaili studies.

This publication comes under category one.

In facilitating these and other publications, the Institute's sole aim is to encourage original, interesting and mature thought, scholarship and analysis of the relevant issues. There will naturally be a diversity of views, ideas and interpretations, and the opinions expressed, will be those of the authors.

Contents

1. Introduction

Over the centuries, great Sufis gifted with spiritual vision have inspired those who encountered them. Their example led to the foundation of spiritual orders that have exerted immense influence on Muslim life and history. Their reflections and poetry have fired the imagination of millions throughout the Muslim world to the present day.

Since the emergence in the second/eighth century of the mystical movement that later came to be known as *taṣawwuf*, Sufi orders have taken myriad shapes and evolved diverse forms of expressions over time and space. Sufi practice, for example, has ranged from ecstatic movement in dance to meditative exercises in quiet solitude. Sufi thought and literature extend from the intense devotional lyrics and spicy aphorisms of poets such as Jalal al-Din Rumi to the elaborate philosophical constructs of individuals such as Ibn al-'Arabi. The fountainhead of Sufism is the promise of enlightenment that offers divinely-graced vision, moral clarity and an encompassing love. These blessings are granted to the individual as a result of a journey within. To the extent that this relies on direct experience rather than cogitation, the mystic journey is anti-rational, and it questions the foundations of standard ethics and ordinary conceptions of reality. Finally, this enlightenment speaks of a dissolution of the very self in a union with the divine that words cannot easily convey.

The role of Sufi orders in the formation of Islamic civilisation from Morocco to Indonesia is fairly well documented. For centuries they were among the most important institutions in Muslim society. They served as centres of learning and poetic creativity, as well as of healing and sanctity. In urban centres these orders were able to recommend spiritual exercises to traders in the bazaar. In rural areas the orders linked trade with spiritual succour and made peace along the fraught boundaries of tribal groupings. In such ways the orders helped knit

1

together vast segments of Islamic civilisation. It may be difficult for many Muslims today to imagine an age when Sufi orders were a pillar of their societies, thoroughly versed in Islamic law, and infusing Muslim piety with inner-directed ethics. For example, until the 19th century, in many parts of the Muslim world, membership in a Sufi order was almost as commonplace as allegiance to a particular school of law.

In recent history, especially in the last century and a half, the Sufis have come under attack for detaining Muslims from grappling with the modern world and from addressing issues of justice and poverty. They have been accused of holding the poor and the ignorant in the thrall of shrines, superstition, other-worldly poetry, and magical and ecstatic practices, at the cost of sober intervention in community problems. Various Muslim groups and organisations blame Sufis for having smuggled into a 'pure' Islam innovations that paralysed reason, imagination and action, and by so doing have contributed to the defeat of the Muslims by the Western empires. Today, many Sufi orders, particularly in the Middle East, have been pushed to the margins of society, surviving mainly in rural areas and among rural migrants in urban settlements.

Modern thought, too, cautions against the mystic impulse. Some contemporary thinkers see in it the temptation to regress from the complex challenges of adult life into child-like certainty. According to such critiques, mysticism gives comfort to those who reject the place of reason in favour of emotion, and shuns the painful choices of daily life. There are numerous examples in current Sufi practices that resonate with such criticisms. In many parts of the Muslim world Sufi dances and chanting are a far cry from the contemplative practices of the great Sufis of the past. Too many Sufis today continue practices such as writing talismanic inscriptions to ward off evil spirits. That is why some Sufis in the West, while upholding the pristine world of quietude and seclusion, poetry and personal enlightenment associated with classical Sufism, reject Sufi orders as forms of organisation contaminated by materiality. The contrast is striking between the spiritual freshness of Jalal al-

Din Rumi's poetry and the crowding that occurs today around his tomb in Konya. The mausoleum has become a museum-cum-shrine, and the whirling dervishes are now packaged as a travelling show. Yet the poetry attributed to him says, 'After we are gone, seek us not in our graves but in the hearts of good people.' These criticisms raise a number of questions about the mystic quest:

(i) To what extent does the mystical path necessitate a withdrawal from the world? Is there a contradiction on the one hand between the demands of contemplation – which include humility, submission and deep suspicion of ordinary human motivation – and on the other the demands of an active, responsible life in the world – which include making difficult choices and exercising one's will to change one's circumstances as well as those of others?
(ii) Is Sufism condemned to serving either as a repository of magical practices among the disenfranchised, or as a personal, individual escape for those better-off in modern life who are merely disillusioned with a life of action and ambition?
(iii) Can Sufism play a role in the modernisation of Muslim society?
(iv) To what extent is the mystical path antagonistic to the demands of the intellect?

This essay is an attempt to grapple with some of these issues, and raise yet others, by examining the situation of the Ismailis of Iran. It is a case-study of apeople whose actions and ideas question, at the very least, the notion that Islamic mysticism is necessarily other-worldly and passive. The community in question brings into focus the dynamic potential of Sufism's other-worldly ideas. While the essay will suggest that there is a place for mystic insight in the very encounter of Muslims with the modern world, such a place has its limits. Indeed, it questions the notion that Muslim life entails submission to any monolithic set of beliefs and practices, be they mystical or legalistic in their formulation.

2. The Ismailis of Iran

One can start with the story of how a particular Muslim community, the Ismailis of Iran, equipped with their Shiʿi faith and a pre-modern form of mysticism, broke away from the fetters of traditional thought and, with determination, set their community on a path to modernity through education and economic development. The research on which this essay is based took place in the late 1970s, when I lived with the Ismailis in Khurasan and conducted over two years of fieldwork.

Ismailism as an historical, intellectual and cultural phenomenon is far more diverse than can be gleaned from research on the Ismailis of Iran. For example, the synthesis achieved during the Fatimid period (909–1171 CE), when great strides were made in Islamic law, science, philosophy, architecture, commerce and technology, is quite distant from the ethos of rural mystics, suffused with Sufi poetry such as that found among the Ismailis of Iran today. Similarly, the rigorous thought of Hasan Sabbah (d.518/1124), with its disciplinarian focus on a hierarchy of adepts, ceased to be a viable model for their religious organisation in Iran after the fall of Alamut to the Mongols and the destruction of its famous library in 654/1256. The Alamut period is for them primarily an image of perseverance and daring – a powerful and heroic image, nonetheless. Finally, the devotional tradition of Indian Ismailism, though closer in tone to the faith of the Iranian Ismailis, employs striking images and melodic themes that are often distinctly Indian. The community of Iranian Ismailis is one segment in the multicultural tapestry of Ismailism.

It will not be possible here to dwell on the history of the Ismailis in Iran.[1] Much of the historical writing on the Iranian Ismailis falls under the shadow cast by the Alamut period; yet this period spans only a small fraction of their history, ending a relatively short interlude of political activism brought about by Hasan Sabbah. Thereafter, the Ismailis retreated from the major arenas of Muslim history. Eventually the *ṭarīqa* became a quietist movement, a phase which lasted five centuries. There are few documents on this period, of which much less can therefore be said. Although the Ismailis are of Shi'i persuasion rather than a Sufi order, for centuries after the fall of Alamut, the Ismaili *ṭarīqa* was suffused with Sufi ideas, poetry and practices. During much of this period in Ismaili history, historians say, it was not easy to point out where Sufism ended and Ismailism began. Their relationship was an inter-permeation of mystical doctrines and spiritual hierarchies.

Despite its political quiescence, the Ismaili community re-consolidated itself to some degree in the 10th/16th century. It spread to populations in India by imaginatively straddling the boundaries of local traditions and tapping a flow of Indian devotional piety. Early in the 13th/19th century, the community became identified clearly under the leadership of their Imams who were known as the Aga Khans.

A crucial juncture for the Iranian Ismailis was the departure of the Imam Hasan 'Ali Shah, Aga Khan I, in 1841 for India after a conflict with the Qajar Shah. From this point on, the community lost physical access to its Imam as well as much of its urban elite, and it appears to have undergone a phase of localised rule that eventually compounded its problems. Local hereditary hierarchies acquired a dominance and, at least in some areas, became cut off from direct contact with the Imam, now based in Bombay. Moreover, the community found itself vulnerable to persecution by local zealots who took advantage of the disorder that plagued Iran early in the century. As one Ismaili put it, 'Those were difficult days. We lost the light of the sun, and had to find our way under the dim light of the moon and the stars.' The community was overwhelmingly rural, with small clusters of settlements in northern and southern Khurasan, around Kirman and Mahallat, near Qum. The *hujjats*, individuals of spiritual rank appointed by the Imam and forming a hierarchy that was tightly organised but supple as a rope, had enabled the community to survive for centuries. But by the end of the 19th and the early part of this century, in many settlements in Iran the structure had become hereditary. This rope came to strangle and choke off direct contact with the person of the Imam, who for almost all Iranian Ismailis had become a mystery.

In the first decades of this century, the 48th Imam of the Ismailis, Sultan Mohammad Shah, Aga Khan III, who assumed his responsibilities at a young age in 1885, decisively began to re-establish direct contact with his community living in the mountain areas of Iran, Afghanistan and elsewhere. He abolished the spiritual hierarchy of the *hujjats*, which had a dramatic effect on the organisation of the community. In doing so he marginalised the local hierarchy by setting up a far more egalitarian structure of authority, yet accountable directly to him. He replaced the hierarchy with positions of limited duration through direct appointment by the Imam. These individuals were given new titles of Indian origin, the *muki* and his assistant the *kamria*. These new peasant leaders, though dedicated and courageous, were far weaker than their erstwhile local lords, and their struggle for legitimacy in the community was inevitably long and painful.

Such was the background to a missive from the Imam Sultan Mohammed Shah at the beginning of the 1930s to his followers in Iran:

> ... I declare that every people and every nation that has truly made an effort in the teaching of modern science has been successful in lifting the shadow of ignorance, giving honour to the faith and the world, and attaining success in the world. [People of faith] must utilise modern science and technology. Thus, it is necessary for the whole community to change their old habits and ways of thinking, In each village you must start a school and send your children where it must be made incumbent on all your children to study.

This was no ordinary modernisation; its impulse radiated from Bombay rather than the West, from a person whose position was profoundly traditional, yet who held views on modern education directly inspired by the success of the West. The Imam gave these peasants the means, and they started by mobilising the village population to obtain land and build the schoolrooms. This was an extremely difficult task owing to opposition, both within the local Ismaili community and beyond.

Fortunately for them, this development roughly coincided with the construction of a modern Iranian nation-state under Reza Shah Pahlavi (1925–41). Ministries and other agencies began to form the infrastructure of a modern state throughout the country. It was astute of the Aga Khan to encourage his followers to take an active role in nation-building under way throughout the country. Their link with the government provided a new buffer against the strong reaction of the local hierarchical elites, a buffer that was to become more resilient in the next generation, as the children of these peasants commenced their education and eventually joined the growing machinery of the provincial bureaucracy, where they thrived.

In the last few decades, anthropologists have uncovered many examples of old potions in new bottles, that is, traditional affiliations taking on new forms. What made this case unusual was that all this school-building was done by peasants, many of them illiterate, who were unable even to imagine the world into which they were to usher their children. Moreover, while education was important to the recently-established Pahlavi dynasty, first priority was given to the urban areas, and within that, to higher education. Hardly a thought was given at that time to the education of young people in the rural areas. Officials in the Ministry of Education must therefore have been surprised to see these Ismaili peasants asking for teachers and books, promising to build their own schools for their children. It is easy to imagine their pleasant surprise when some of these farmers later added that they wanted to educate not just their sons but also their daughters. Although education was theoretically aimed at both sexes, in peasant communities it was rare at that time.

How the Ismailis went about to attain their educational goal and what happened thereafter is predictable. Primary schools were started during the 1940s and 1950s in many Ismaili settlements in Khurasan, Kirman and the Mahallat areas. By the early 1970s Dizbad, one of the first villages to build a school in the

1940s, was given the accolade of being the first in Iran to achieve 100 per cent literacy. There was even a seventy-year old woman in another village in northern Khurasan who had learned to read and write. The students eventually obtained higher education in urban areas and stayed on to form a new generation that was an urban, educated elite. By the late 1960s there emerged whole cohorts of young Ismailis who had become – mainly – teachers and health officers, with a sprinkling of doctors and military officials. For example, in Mashhad these recent migrants to the city established a highly successful co-operative which enabled them to purchase their own homes. This urbanised, technocratic elite gradually consolidated, and eventually came to form the backbone of the new leadership.

3. The Paradox of World-affirming Mysticism

The results of this modernisation are the most obvious part of the story. Less obvious, but no less important, was the transformation that must have taken place in the minds of the farmers themselves – in their medieval, mystical world-view, atrophied by a long period of steady decline in rural isolation. What in this tradition enabled them to embrace the modern world with such enthusiasm? Their conception of human nature was premodern, drawing on Graeco–Muslim thought as it had percolated through the Muslim world over the centuries. Their poetry was full of intense religious longing and love, far from the materiality of a frail and inconstant daily life.

It bears repeating that these Ismailis were peasants, and therefore anxiously dependent on a nature that was fickle, and on a political economy that was far beyond their influence. Their ideas and experiences resonated with their understanding of the elements, the rhythm of nature and the cycle of life; their knowledge of the human body and its parts. Their beliefs about the spirit world and ultimate reality, in turn, fitted into that larger picture. Yet out of their love poetry and the arcane and sometimes untamed exegeses of Qur'anic tales, these peasants fashioned a coherent conceptual engine for the transformation of their community into modernity.

It is a poignant irony that most of their children and grandchildren, who enjoyed the fruits of their commitment to education, today know only fragments of the world-view of their parents and grandparents, and accept little of what they do know of it. This bespeaks the depth of the transformation that the Ismaili peasants had engendered. They carried their young down an arduous path to a shore from which the children left for the domains of modern knowledge unknowable to their rural parents. All the peasants knew was that the acquisition of this knowledge was important to the future of their children who must study and do well at it. These boys and girls later returned forever changed, their training vindicated by the positions that began to open up to them in the government.

However, though the older generation gave due credit to the benefits of modern knowledge, they would often contrast the literal attitude of the recently educated Iranians to religious thought with that of their great ancestors – the poets and theological rhetoricians who possessed the insight to grasp mystical poetry and understand multiple layers of meaning. It is to these insights that we now turn.

4. Windows to an Understanding

How does one come to grips with something as complex as the religious thought of a community? A useful beginning is to look at how concepts are lived and understood through life. Locating the role of thought in the fullness and complexity of life is not a simple matter. Beyond certain basics, it will not take us very far to look for Iranian Ismaili thought in the abstract as a single doctrinal system. What an idea is cannot be separated totally from where in life it is located, that is, among those who hold interpretations and where and how these interpretations are made. In other words, a proper understanding of Iranian Ismailism lies not in the texts themselves, or even among those who, by virtue of their formal study of the texts, claim authority over the doctrine. Rather, it is found among a number of individuals who, by virtue of their reading, their understanding, their interest in religious debate and their passion for poetry, have come to command the respect of the community. These ideas are distributed among ordinary people in less sophisticated and more formulaic language, but they serve as a foundation for their identity and their actions as Ismailis. In sum, these are ideas that reside somewhere between the stillness of the text and the ever-moving, daily consciousness of ordinary people.

What sorts of ideas are they? They can be explicit, such as beliefs about who the Ismailis are as human beings and as adherents to a faith, what their history is, and what distinguishes right from wrong. Or they can be more tacit, residing quietly, but no less importantly, in the assumptions and practices of the devout. These practices can be of prayer and religious devotion, can pertain to cleanliness, purity, illness and health, or can mark and make sense of the cycle of life, including birth, coming of age, marriage and death.

While this essay will expound on their doctrine or concept of human nature, it must not be mistaken for 'the basic doctrines of Iranian Ismailism.' To do so is to commit a fallacy that such a conception is the oral equivalent of a written philosophy, and that it is somehow one thing for everyone. Such monolithic fantasies are all too prevalent among Muslims today. Iranian Ismaili doctrine is more like the branches of a tree with roots in the imagery and narratives of the Qur'an, *ḥadīth* and the lives and teachings of the Imams: each branch grows this way and that, each springs from a unique place in the tree, each diverges in its strategy to capture light through its myriad leaves; yet the leaves are identical and the branches are of a type that, when taken together, all form the tree itself.

There are four occasions when such ideas come to the surface or find tacit expression in ritual. Roughly in order, from the public to the private, they are as follows:

(i) Pilgrimages. These are regular journeys made to sacred sites by large numbers of people from the surrounding area, as well as from other parts of the country.

(ii) Discussions, debates and conflicts. More spontaneous, but no less public, these take place in a variety of settings, at funerals, at home and in the village.

(iii) Formal pronouncements. Speeches and sermons by intellectual leaders to the community in settings such as the jama'at-khana (community hall).

(iv) Coteries of interpretation. This domain is much more private, wherein individuals or small groups in intimate settings interpret poetry and discuss variances of meaning.

5. The Pilgrimage

Of the public rituals of the community, the grandest are the regular pilgrimages that all the people from surrounding villages undertake together with their relatives and friends from the city, be they Ismaili or Ithna'ashari.[2] These are large-scale, jovial processions and form an important point in the annual cycle of village life – a local, though distant, echo of the *ḥajj*. The processions culminate at the sacred site marked by a tomb, a spring, a tree, or a combination of the three. Once the pilgrims arrive, the mood changes to one of ritual solemnity or intensity, corresponding to the site which is usually spectacular, perched high up in a remote valley.

In many villages there are local pilgrimages to sacred sites, and I will describe two, one each from northern and southern Khurasan respectively. The first is the larger and better-known, to a site called Naw Hisar, near the village of Dizbad. The second, more of a local affair, but no less important to the villages involved, is to a site near the village of Gulunabad in the area of Birjand.

5.1 The Pilgrimage to Naw Hisar

This pilgrimage takes place every year during a transition period after the summer, but before the harvest of plums which is an important source of village income. The event also takes place just as the educated members of the community return to the towns and cities from their holidays. Among them are teachers, medical officials and government employees, who originate in the village but now work in the urban areas of Iran. Scores of cars come, mainly from the city of Mashhad a few hours away, and the nearby town of Nishapur, as well as from distant Tehran. The pilgrimage takes place, therefore, during a time of family reunion and communal in-gathering.

The whole day is devoted to the pilgrimage which starts early in the morning, when the villagers load their donkeys with rugs, samovars and foodstuffs, with some sheep trailing. The pilgrimage begins without ceremony, with groups going by this route or that, in an informal, jocular atmosphere. The jokes exchanged by the young men can even be ribald. The children, most excited, race ahead, climbing along the higher ridges, chasing and daring one another. Between 9 and 10 am, people reach a levelled area strewn with trees, about 12 km away from the village. This is not yet Naw Hisar, strictly speaking. It is the penultimate resting place, at which everybody has breakfast, forming a vast picnic amidst the mottled shadows cast by the trees. Slowly the various families gather, numbering over 1,000 people. In recent years the numbers of pilgrims have reportedly swelled enormously.

Just after breakfast, an air of quiet resolve descends. A few people start to get up and move off. The old and bent seem as determined as the young, who weave around them and take more tricky paths higher up. They file upwards along a sharply rising valley. Suddenly, around a bend, the site comes into view at the end of the valley, a stony collar that stretches magnificently several hundred feet up. Its undulations command the entire valley, forming a giant amphitheatre of scree. The focal point of the site is not a stage, but a dense clump of trees. Nothing else grows.

The first person to get to the site sacrifices a goat or sheep in the name of the whole village. Others may also do this. The pilgrims gather around the trees, some squatting, and others, mainly women, huddling busily next to it. Beside the women is a rippling spring, with people bending over to drink from its cool, clear, almost icy water as it emerges into the brilliant sunshine. The spring slakes more than a thirst for water. On a ledge of slate just above the spring the women burn cotton-wool soaked in oil and from the sticky residue they smear their eyelids and eyelashes as well as those of their children. This spring is regarded as *tabarruk*, a source of blessings. Soon the gathering becomes large, as people squat or sit on the area in front of the trees and upon the rising scree, the men settling down on the left, the women on the right. One man stands up to explain why they are all gathered:

> Imamquli was greatly drawn to spiritual matters, even when he was a little boy, far too young to be allowed in for communal prayers. One day Imam Abu'l-Hasan 'Ali Shah was visiting. When food was being distributed to the congregation after the prayers, the Imam pointed at the ceiling and said, 'Give the little one up there his share of the food.' People were puzzled and someone climbed up to the roof. They caught the little boy peering down to listen to the prayers and gave him the food.
>
> One night, a few years later, the boy Imamquli was sitting among the women who were spinning cotton while they recited poetry in praise of the imam called *ḥaqqani*, which he loved to hear. The boy suddenly noticed the Imam passing by the door on his horse. All the women were oblivious of this, but the young boy dashed out, grabbed the Imam's cloak and held onto his bridle. He walked with the Imam and insisted that the Imam grant him his *murād* or spiritual wish. The Imam dismissed him, saying, 'You are a child.' The boy said, 'I am qualified for my wish.' The Imam said, 'You will attain your goal when your beard is thick enough for a comb to get stuck in it' [that is, when you are old enough].
>
> Imamquli refused to give up and continued to badger the Imam. The Imam threw his whip some distance away, told Imamquli to return it to him, and went on riding. Imamquli grabbed it in the dark and it turned into the head of a dragon. He ignored the fangs, raced back to the Imam and returned it, whereupon it

turned back into a whip. The Imam then threw his walking-stick on the ground and told the boy to return it. As Imamquli reached down to pick it up, it turned into a snake. This did not deter the boy, who picked it up and gave it back to the Imam, whereupon it turned back into a stick.[3]

By now they had reached a particular spot about a mile upriver from the village of Dizbad, where today two streams meet. The Imam struck a stone with his stick and water sprung forth. The Imam thought to himself, 'This ought to satisfy the boy.' But it didn't and the Imam made to hasten ahead of the stubborn boy. The boy followed him until they reached Naw Hisar, right here where we now are. The Imam then pointed to a rock and told the boy to carry it up over the mountain ahead of them. This the boy did and returned. The Imam then struck a rock and a spring of the coldest water in Khurasan spurted forth. Again he thought this would satisfy the boy.

However, when Imamquli tugged at him more, the Imam finally and impatiently said, 'Whenever a comb gets stuck in your beard I will grant you your wish.' Imamquli said, 'Give me your comb.' He got it and thrust it into his hairless cheek until it sank into the flesh.

> O you the ignorant!
> Have you any idea what happened
> ... or what didn't?
> The murīd got his murād.
> Know any more
> ... we just couldn't.

Imamquli then returned to the women, who had never missed him because to them no time had passed since the boy saw the Imam. From that day on Imamquli became a great poet and the most famous ancestor of the people of Dizbad.[4]

The narrative over, the pilgrims, now hushed, break into a recital of ecstatic verses from Jalal al-Din Rumi's *Dīvān-i Shams-i Tabrīz*. The crowd then gets up, and returns to the picnic ground. Many sheep, sacrificed to thank God for granting a wish, are cut up into small pieces and dropped in the numerous pots of a delicious Iranian stew called *ābgūsht*. As the women prepare this late lunch, the families sit in clutches on the richly-coloured, sun-dappled rugs and enjoy tea. Numbers of people flit from group to group and catch up on one another in a round of easy informality that nevertheless carefully obeys the order of seniority: a junior relative or friend visits the senior, and a villager the guest. After the lunch, everyone streams along various routes back to the village.

5.2 The Pilgrimage to Abalu

This pilgrimage, which takes place in the spring, also attracts pilgrims from several villages of different Shi'i communities. It is the tomb of Darvish Qutb al-Din, a poet strongly linked to the village of Yahn in Gulnabad, southern Khurasan, who was said to have attained great heights of spirituality and learning, and then withdrew to live up in the hills. It is therefore a shrine rather than a natural site. Here, as well, the atmosphere at the start is jocular as the streams of pilgrims, young and old, edu-cated teachers and farmers, make their various ways from the surrounding villages. The tomb is a humble structure but, perched high up a bluff, it enjoys a commanding view of the dusty plains far below and the valleys that lead up to it. Pil-grims enter, crouch next to the sarcophagus and, touching it with their right index finger, utter a silent prayer. They then move around it to the exit. It takes a minute or so for each individual, and there are about six or seven there at any one time. In a few hours, all the pilgrims have performed this cer-emony, their *ziyārat* to the saint.

Below the precipice that edges the tomb is a softly sloping hill dotted with deep red rugs that the families start to unroll as they gather to set up their fires and cooking pots to prepare a meal. Sheep are sacrificed in the traditional Muslim fashion, again the result of a vow in fulfillment of an answered *ḥājat* or need. As in Naw Hisar, individuals drift from one family to an-other to greet and ask after them. Throughout this time, a steady trickle of women huddle busily by a spring called Abalu, hidden in a nick in the hill right below the picnickers. Here too, they light cotton-wool and rub its black residue around the eyes of their children in the hope of preventing the evil eye.

After the meal, atop the roof of a building adjacent to the spring, a loud drumming heralds the insistent wail of a reed instrument called the *nay*. Men, both young and old, respond to the call, skip down the dust and stones, and start a vigorous dance. On the roof of a mud brick building, in full view of the entire crowd, they spin and circle in unison to the 5/8 rhythm of the drum and the seductive cry of the *nay*. They pull out and wave their scarves, crouch, then jump up, as a cart-wheel that rises and falls again. This lasts for an hour or two, during which some tire and others replace them. As the dance winds down, people start to pack up and make their way home, forming speckled filaments that branch off and wind along the paths that descend slowly into the villages.

What is the significance of these pilgrimages? Through these traditions, in word and deed, people make four statements about the inner life, time, divine intervention and society.

5.3 The Primacy of the Mystic Quest

The figures commemorated at the centre of these pilgrimages attained their mystic quest. The story of Imamquli is replete with reminders of how only the daring, the undistractable and the persistent will attain their spiritual goals. The initial kindness of the Imam to the boy hiding on the roof of the prayer-hall turns to supreme indifference when the lad starts to show an interest in undertaking the spiritual journey. The Imam's symbols of authority turn into dreadful animals and his expressions of spiritual power cause water to spout from rock, thus signifying that power, authority and riverine miracles are worldly temptations the Imam throws at you to test your resolve to attain the ultimate goal which lies well beyond the matters of this world. This spiritual journey requires not just tenacity but self-mutilation, that is, personal sacrifice. In the example from southern Khurasan, although less is said about Darvish Qutb al-Din, he became a figure for the whole region, because when he attained spiritual greatness he left the confines of his own village. At their simplest, these figures are a reminder of the riches awaiting those who start this difficult journey, riches in poetry and action that will resound for centuries thereafter.

5.4 *The Consecration of History*

In both cases the pilgrimage evokes the history of the community through its great ancestors: the tale of the young Imamquli at the site where he attained his spiritual goal, and the life and spiritual rank of Darvish Qutb al-Din embodied in the reverence of his tomb. Both these characters embody the local history of the community, or to put it another way, they localise the community's history. The sacrifice of the sheep locates the Ismailis in the tradition of the Prophet Ibrahim and thus on the larger canvas of Muslim sacred history; the story told and the poetry chanted anchor the community to its unique history. The power of the site emanates from the miracle of water. Thus is nature spiritualised and the spirit naturalised. Were it not for such traditions, this local history would have evaporated in rural obscurity during the harsh, mostly undocumented centuries after the fall of Alamut. The site becomes a book, the pilgrimage its reading and rereading. Nothing can obliterate such a book other than a natural catastrophe or the complete annihilation of a community.[5]

5.5 *The Cohabitation of Diverse Meanings*

Imamquli's quest is at the centre of the pilgrimage to Naw Hisar. But there is a profound contradiction inherent in the events consecrated: on the one hand, if you follow your heart you reach a height greater than any to be found on earth; on the other hand, if you burn cotton-wool and utter a prayer over it, the black residue will protect your child from the evil eye. The contradiction is quite clear in the story: Imamquli refused to be deterred by miracles of gushing water. Yet both ideas coexist like very different plants fed by the same stream, each nourished by the site. The fact that springs are involved in both the pilgrimages is interesting: the water not only gushes forth in a miraculous event, but water is needed and used by all; its grace is rendered universal by the vitality it gives to life.

This cohabitation of meanings has major implications for the identity of the community. The pilgrimage connects the unique and historically momentous event of one man's spiritual attainment to the daily grind of ordinary life. In other words, it conjoins the charismatic with the routine; the grace of spiritual vision is offered to the few and some protection from the risks of daily life to others. This coexistence is not entirely successful, and the tension buried in the diversity of meanings can rise to the surface. For example, a number of individuals, both educated and the more radically mystical, set fire to a shrine to the horror of many villagers, as we shall see later. Nevertheless, we can note here that thousands of pilgrims go to the more important sites, where those who are sceptical of magical practices, either from a political or a mystical point of view, line up or sit next to those who revere the site in their simple way. This coexistence speaks volumes of the capacity of the site to encompass and contain such diversity of perspectives.

5.6 Structure and Antistructure

It is important to note that the Naw Hisar and Abalu pilgrimages are the only sacred occasions on which adherents of both Shiʿi communities, of all ages and from all the nearby villages, as well as their urbanised offspring gather. These pilgrimages evoke and reinforce the solidarity of a fragile community – a community emerging in and through the pilgrimage that in normal times is quite divergent, sometimes even in conflict. Sacred places in nature have the advantage over religious buildings in an urban area in that they are open to the sky and offer access to all who wish to go there. It is significant that in Abalu, members of both the Shiʿi communities claim Darvish Qutb al-Din for their own.[6]

There is meaning in the movement as well. Jocularity among separated parties begins a journey that culminates when they gather at a place. The spot is away from the everyday concerns of life, away from structure and from everything that bounds human beings and separates one from the other. It is a place with charisma, in that it offers a tangible link with what is considered to be the good and the ultimate truth. Yet if we consider how food is dealt with, we see that the rituals feed two divergent messages: the single sheep sacrificed by the first person at the site is sacrificed in the name of all, yet there is no communal cooking or eating. Each family cooks their own meal, invites others and thus demarcates structure; that is, each family reinforces the fixed pattern of relationships in which rules of rank, standards of consumption, obligation and reciprocation all work to establish where human beings differ from one another and how they relate to one another.

Thus, in the pilgrimage to Naw Hisar, the sacrifice recalls the event that unites all Muslims, the willingness of Ibrahim to sacrifice his beloved son Ismail. At the same time, the event respects the lines that establish the structures of ordinary life. The activities at Abalu are also linked to the important celebrations of Nawruz, which I have described and analysed elsewhere.[7]

Where does this narrative take us in grasping how the Ismailis of Iran understood modernisation in the late 1970s? These pilgrimages illustrate how a vision so powerful as to propel a community through such a difficult transformation is anchored in community life. The pilgrimage affirms not only the ultimate goal of spiritual life, but also that this goal is worth pursuing in the face of the immense difficulties along the way. These practices do not reveal much about the nature of the social transformation, but they are essential as a setting for spiritual transformation by underlining its importance as well as the fortitude required for the difficult journey. The pilgrimage lends focus to the spiritual heart of the community, the eternal fixedness of the spiritual centre, around which all else may change. This idea, while it is tacit here, finds a voice in the

explicit statements by the community to itself, as we shall dis-
cover later. We must first turn to situations in which members
of the community present their views on faith and life to others.

6. The World of Debates

One of the recurring features of Iranian culture is the fond-
ness for lively debate on serious matters. When the issue hinges
on the nature of time or progress, or human nature or responsibility, such conversations, debates and confrontations set the
boundary of the community of the faithful. Here, the voices of
the community are more strident, declamatory and definitive.
The message is, 'Here we differ from the others.' The Ismailis
say that they are the people of allegorical interpretation (*ahl-i
ta'wīl*), not of literalist imitation (*ahl-i taqlīd*). They argue that
the true meaning of Muslim religious practices (*furū'-i din*) is
that they serve as analogues for the inner life. Thus, the inner
significance of the *hajj* is that of the journey to the spirit within
us; ablution means the inner purity of motivation; the fast of
Ramadhan an abstention from lying, gossip, envy and theft;
and holy war is the *jihād-i akbar*, the greater struggle, the inner,
ethical combat against one's own baser instincts. This empha-
sis on *ta'wīl* does not, of course, negate the requirements of
exoteric practices. It is perhaps ironical that at the local level,
the Ismailis often contrasted their affinity with mystical thought
and allegory against the literalist approach of their Twelver
neighbours, since historically speaking, Shi'ism and Sufism
have been closely associated, and a number of senior Twelver
'ulamā' have long shown a predilection for mystic imagery in
their thought and poetry.

A second theme of self-presentation is that the mystics want
to taste the actualities of spiritual insight rather than to settle
for the mere promise of heaven or security from hell in the
afterlife. As one Ismaili put it, 'We want to encounter the reality of the spirit here and now, not to wait and wait for heaven;
we want cash, not a promissory note.' To them, heaven and
hell symbolise spiritual states rather than places, the former

representing the soul's union with the divine and the latter its separation from God.[8]

A third theme is that the potential for union with the divine is universal. During a funeral, a villager happened to mention that only Muslims have souls. An Ismaili mystic immediately retorted, 'If that is the case, how come Edison invented so many things, and how come so much science was developed in the West?' This man in his forties, who had not had the benefit of high-school education, felt strongly enough about this episode to recount it again and again. Its significance is the assumption, commonly held among the Ismailis, that the source of all great achievements in rationality and technology is the spirit within.

7. Formal Pronouncements

In the formal pronouncements of a community we find the most official, most formal and most general view of its principles and ideals. In this domain resides the community's self-presentation. Such statements represent the core beliefs of the community by saying, 'Here we stand.' Being formal, this domain does not usually reveal the fissures of meaning that are found within every community of believers; neither can it explore the rich veins of individual interpretation within Ismaili esotericism, as we shall examine later.

Mulla Shams al-Din, an elderly and highly respected leader among his fellow-farmers, had a history of spiritual adventure and public service. As a young man in the 1930s, he had undergone an experience that, in his words, opened his inner eye to the higher realities and gave him powers of prescience, both of which, he noted with disappointment, were now dimmed. Nevertheless, his credibility in the local community was vital to the young educated leaders who had just been appointed by the Aga Khan IV to head the Ismaili community in the early 1970s. Individuals such as he were able to mobilise the support of the rural members of the community. In the following example, he had accompanied the young leaders to a village in order to encourage the farmers to contribute towards the building of hostels for boys and girls in the nearby town of Birjand. The hostels were for those children who were having difficulty in finding reasonable accommodation in the town while attending school:

> ... The bricks of the eternal are built in this world. We must all co-operate and work together. To know the Lord is first to know ourselves. When we know the self, we will know why we came to this world. Until we reach the Ultimate Truth, we will always have doubt. When we shake hands after prayer and pray for the vision of the Lord, we see the vision within one another. The veil between us and our Lord is our action. Our spirit, however, has been given birth from the command of the Ultimate. One should not have pride. Worship is nothing save service to mankind. We should have purity of intent. Life without good works is worthless. The heart must be pure and unveiled. Our Lord said that He is in the heart of the believers.[9] Good works are the bricks of the building of faith. The lower self must be extinguished. Giving of oneself to build this hostel will help lift the veils of self-conceit that lie between you and the spirit within.

What is so interesting about these remarks is how tightly human action binds the spiritual to the material worlds, so that it is impossible to separate the two. Moreover, Mulla Shams did not rest his plea on a simple pragmatic rationale – that to build the hostel will bring educational benefits to their children. Metaphysics rather than instrumental reason provides the ultimate reason for action; the rationale for co-operation resides in the inner life. Action is a means toward a metaphysical end, a purpose that is entirely other-worldly, yet cannot be separated from a this-worldly endeavour.[10] What thinking, what understanding of the world, of the self and of our ultimate fate lies behind this simple remark?

7.1 *The Creation of Humanity*

Interestingly enough, Mulla Shams al-Din was also the most eloquent about the origination of humanity. Here is his tale of the creation of Adam as he narrated it to me during an interview:

> The coming of humanity to this world is to recognise [God] the Maintainer. When, on the first day, a command was given to angel Gabriel, then to angel Israfil and finally to Izra'il to bring clay to make Adam, rivalry ensued between them. Based on how they performed this task, they would be arrayed in rows of different ranks according to how close they were to God. God ordered Gabriel to collect clay from the four pillars of the world. When Gabriel took the soil, it cried out, saying, 'I cannot accept the divine test.' So the angel relented and dropped the soil. Similarly, Israfil failed to bring the soil. Izra'il, on the other hand, was firmer. He said that there is no going back on God's command; the soil must fulfill its duty.
>
> After Izra'il brought the soil, God praised him and said that his ability not to be fooled by the soil entitled him to perform the exalted task of bringing the spirit to Adam. He was thus the closest angel to God.
>
> Gabriel was then commanded to make Adam from the four elements – soil, air, fire and water. Gabriel asked, ' In what form should I make Adam?' God said, 'Fill a bowl with water and look at [the reflection of] My face.' The spirit was ordered to enter the frame of Adam.
>
> God then told the angels, 'Whoever wants to recognise My Unity must bow to Adam.' Those of the first rank recognised that the essence of the Maintainer was breathed into Adam. They paid their respects – as we do in our prayers; we bow to the same spirit [within us] that was breathed into Adam on the first day. The first row was the Row of Unity. They gave witness to the Unity of God and were not sent to the world. The second row comprised those who partly doubted and those who partly recognised [the Divine Unity]. They were ordered to enter the world and were called the People of the Firmament, and whichever of them recognised the Unity would join the first row. The third row were of those who could have worshipped the spirit, but chose to worship clay. They were called the Ranks of Contrariety. They are damned to [a life of] ignorance and lowly existence.

A notable feature of this narrative is the tension that appears in all the three stages of the drama of creation: the primordial unity of man in God; the unification of spirit and matter in the act of creation; and the final recognition of, and obeisance to, Adam.

(i) The creation of Adam signifies in a sense the departure of the soul from its state of pre-eternal unity with God. Many Ismailis speak of this unity as the ocean from which man, the droplet of water, has become separate. If properly guided, the confluence of the droplets of the faithful will form the river, and finally join the ocean from which it had originally sprung. This separation is not just a fact of existence, but provides the basis for human purpose on earth, for just as a droplet longs for a return to the ocean, so the human being is drawn towards God.

(ii) Matter endures the stress of two tensions, one within and the other without. On the one hand, there is a tension between the independence and the submission of matter, between matter as an end, expressed in its willful and cunning self-preoccupation, and matter as a means, as shown by its capacity to contain the spirit and become its instrument. On the other hand, there is a tension between the worship of spirit and the worship of matter, the clay that houses the spirit. The former leads to union with God, while the latter leads to ignorance, contrariety and damnation. When God commanded the angels to pay homage to Adam, He set in motion the drama of history, the coexistence and tension between those who are aware of the possibility of reunion with the divine and those who know of no such thing. This tension is clearly situated in the choice that human beings must continually make in the course of their lives:

> Gar kunad mayl-i ān buvad bih az ān,
> Gar kunad mayl-i in buvad pas az in.

> If he takes to that, he rises above all else there;
> If he takes to this, he plummets below all else here.

From the very beginning, the alliance of spirit and matter has been uneasy: matter must be collected from disparate

places. This task calls for the diligence, watchfulness and stead-
fastness of the angels, for matter resists the awesome
responsibility of the divine test. The spirit, on the other hand,
descends by a simple act of self-reflection into the body of Adam.
There is thus a tense coexistence between the spirit, originally
unitary but temporarily separated, and matter, originally disparate though now combined in the form of man.

These tensions, contained in the story of creation, are a
genetic code, as it were, of many components of Ismaili thought.
The first tension establishes the longing of humanity to return
to God and also explains why human beings differ from one
another: each individual is apportioned a different share of
earth, air, fire and water. Self-knowledge leads to reunion with
the divine, and matter must become the instrument for that
return. The second tension relates to two fundamentally distinct modes of religious life, the *ẓāhir* (exoteric) and the *bāṭin*
(esoteric), which interpenetrate yet differ fundamentally from
each other. This distinction helps us understand how the
Ismailis embraced modernisation by differentiating yet con-
necting the two dimensions: the outer, the contingent and the
constantly changing, and the inner, the essential and the eter-
nally unchanging.

7.2 Self-Knowledge

The fundamental problem for the Ismailis is based on the question, '*insān chīst?*' (What does it mean to be a human?).[11] For
the mystic, such a question penetrates the contingent in man
to the spirit within which, as we have seen, he originates from
God and longs to return to Him. The Ismailis see this question
as the beginning of knowledge of oneself (*khud shināsī*). What
is tacit is the notion that most people under normal worldly
conditions, or in what they call the outer (*ẓāhirī*) form of religious life, are unaware of the spirit within man. In such a state
of ignorance, they prefer to worship God as an entity beyond
the reach of personal apprehension, accessible to them merely
through the physical reminders of His existence. How does

one escape the ignorance of the spirit that dwells within each
one of us? The Ismailis interviewed often quote the saying of
the Prophet Muhammad: *man 'arafa nafsahu faqad 'arafa
rabbahu* (he who knows himself knows his Lord), or cite the
following lines:

> Tu kih dar khud shinākhtan ʿājiz,
> kay shināsi khudaya-rā hargiz?

> If you do not know yourself,
> when will you ever know your Lord?[12]

7.3 Individual Transformation and Community

Now we come closer to a perception of how the Ismailis gave
forward historical momentum to mysticism. Self-knowledge is
a process, not a moment, and it moves in three directions: inward, forward and upward. In addition to and opposed to these
movements, the Ismailis refer to other dispositions in terms of
outward, backwards, and low or remaining behind. Perhaps
the most explicit and comprehensive account of this conception that I came across was given by a missionary who preached
this sermon in a village *jamā 'at-khāna*:

> The faith in the *ẓāhir* and the *bāṭin* was a circle, an enclosure full
> of divine wisdom and bounty. It was a law from creation brought
> down to humanity. This enclosure was for both the general and
> the elect, but the elect were more inclined towards it. Its source
> was before Prophet Adam and before Prophet Muhammad, but it
> was perfected on the day of Ghadir-i Khumm when the last verse
> of the Qur'an was revealed. The Prophet said, 'For those who
> accept Islam, today I have perfected your religion and you must
> follow it.'[13] We are in such a circle, within the parapets of wisdom
> which is an inheritance from that day, and we are companions of
> the higher truth.
>   Islam [is the faith of] one who has submitted to the command
> [of God], one who is a mediator, one who loves his fellows ... One
> who submits to Islam must choose brotherhood, equality, progress,
> amplitude [of spirit], knowledge, all of that ... Our ancestors and
> the greatest among us put into practice the prayer that was recited

in the days of the Prophet. It has been a ladder, a few rungs of which we have climbed. The community is moving on its own, it is progressing and developing. We are moving. We have not come into this world to remain in one place. O brothers and sisters, if we consider the actualities and submit to Islam, we must behave according to the orders of the Imam. The Qur'an says, 'O peaceful souls, your actions should be pure so that you are content with yourselves and God is content with you.'[14]

The law that Adam had, Noah did not have; Moses did not have the law that Noah was given; Jesus did not have the law that Moses had. That is, with the passing of time, it [the law] was perfected; step by step it was amended. As I pointed out, the community is part of the auxiliaries of the faith (*furū '-i din*), and it is going forward, it is not in decline. Just as we are small [in childhood] and grow big, so our clothing, our food, like our religion, changes appropriately; it progresses, it accumulates wisdom.

Let us briefly explore the imagery of this homily. The first and most obvious feature is that of movement – the movement of divine wisdom onto the arena of history, the movement of history itself, accumulating wisdom as it goes, the transmutation of the divine prescriptions introduced by the Prophets. The sermon continued:

The *sharī 'at* (religious law) is the beginning of things. If we imagine an almond, the flower is fertilised, the seed grows big and develops a skin. This skin is the beginning of the task. Its purpose is to allow the inner shell and the nut within it to grow big. Then we slowly reach the *ṭarīqat* (path), which we must practice. We then continue to the *ḥaqīqat* (higher truth), which is the Imam himself [with whose help] we see God with our inner eye. But the *ma 'rifat* (the highest realm of knowledge) of God is something else – it is the essence that drips from the flesh of the almond ... one must struggle enormously to attain the Light that is hidden within God.

Here, again, the imagery is all of movement: upwards in the ascent of the elect towards the truth of gnosis, which is symbolised by the steady growth of the almond from seed to stone-fruit; and inwards in his progression from shell to seed, culminating in the formation of the oil of the almond, the precious bounty

of the highest knowledge. The stages of spiritual development
– *sharī'at*, *ṭarīqat*, *ḥaqīqat* and *ma'rifat* – combine both inward
and upward movement. They are contained one within the
other like the layers of the almond nut; but they are also ranked
one above the other like the steps of a ladder which one climbs,
from one horizon to another. The highest practice, that of the
recollection (*zikr*) of the Names of God, is regarded as 'the
heart of the heart of the heart.' The preacher ended with the
following remarks on the role of the community:

> Our community is separated according to levels, not according to
> one's age, but according to *ma'rifat*. A few people are in a higher
> category. We must understand that we have travelled and are
> travelling along a path. The Imam says, 'If you are in the first
> rank, you must be inspired by the second rank.' All of us are each
> other's teachers; we are mirrors for one another. It is not as if
> each person leaves his own house and returns to his own house.
> No, we have an abundance of responsibilities. Just as we have
> responsibilities in this world, we have responsibilities for the next.
> We are from one family. Although our impress is different, our
> spirit is one. We are the children of the same father and mother.

The implications of the sermon for social commitment are
fairly easy to draw out. Here, like Mulla Shams, the speaker
intertwined individual insight and community responsibility.
In the inter-reflection of the members of the community, each
one is to be a mirror for the other, each one seeing in the
other a self-reflective, ethical conscience. This is a process that
sheds the differences which divide and brings the community
closer for the final return to God.

Time and timelessness are related through a powerful com-
posite image of that which is within, that which encloses, and
the remainder without. The image is not linear but circular,
and within it movement does not occur. It is perfected, an in-
heritance that is permanent. It encloses and protects those who
are steadfast within the limits of its wisdom. Thus, stasis and
movement, eternal and contingent, inner and outer, are both
in the individual and in history. Progress is at once made within
the individual and without in the community. Ethical action

links the two levels, bringing about union with God on the one level and progression in history on the other. Finally, the community provides the mirror for self-recognition, an essential process of the journey to be undertaken.

We now move to situations in which selected individuals within the community articulate the faith in the most private domain, forming coteries.

8. The Coteries of Interpretation

The settings for coteries can be semi-private, as in the *jamā ʿat-khāna*, where the faithful offer prayers as Ismailis, or private, or sometimes even secret, within the four walls of the home. Discussions are often based on the readings or recitations of the great poets that these Ismailis consider the leading lights of their tradition – Jalal al-Din Rumi, Saʿdi, Hafiz, Omar Khayyam, Khaki Khurasani, to name but a few.

In these sessions, what counts is the ability to understand the different levels of meaning in a text or recitation; the economic or educational backgrounds of the participants are irrelevant. However, since human beings are unequal in their capacity to understand these layers of meaning, interpretation itself must adjust to the context. The presence of the literal-minded determines the semantic context of the group because literalism poses greater dangers.[15]

The clarification of meaning is therefore protected by careful respect for context: one is tested, often invisibly. This cautious sensitivity is more refined than a simple desire for secrecy, and is not to be confused with the practice of *taqiyya*, which is to be circumspect with beliefs when the situation is dangerous. A much more subtle layering of meaning is involved here. The Ismailis call this process *ta ʾwīl*, from the Arabic *awwal* or 'first'. *Ta ʾwīl* occurs when the meaning of a doctrine, story or ritual is restored to its first or original sense through allegorical or symbolic hermeneutics.

In the *jamā ʿat-khāna* one evening, an older Ismaili recited the poetry of Hafiz, the famous Persian poet whom they claim was an Ismaili, as they tend to do with all the great poets they admire:

> [God says:] The secret of the wages for My love
> is that the lovers draw every bit of suffering I mete.
> I sent Adam from Heaven
> so that he would respect My power.
> I saved Noah from the Flood
> as I made the hands of Moses white.

The poem is about the suffering God inflicts on those He most loves as the price for their attainment of His love. As the reciter went through each line, describing the tribulations of the prophets, he exercised his allegorical imagination, giving his interpretation (*ta'wīl*) of the inner (*bāṭin*) meaning implied in each case. Although the other prophets were discussed, it was Noah who received particular attention. Perhaps this was because more than any other prophet, the lengthy isolation of Noah during his mission and the small number of those saved from the Flood offers an image more resonant with the circumstances of the Iranian Ismailis.

8.1 The Background to Figuration

The interpreter first gave the background, that is, a literal rendering of the story of Noah as given in the Qur'an:[16] the 950 years Noah preached in vain; the signs of the Flood; the disobedience of his son; his reproach to God for having allowed his son to drown; and God's response that in disobeying God's will, Noah's son had forfeited his family. That is the literal meaning of the story as factual narrative, or the myth in its outer (*ẓāhirī*) form.[17]

8.2 The Allegory of the Community

The interpreter then gave his *ta'wīl* of the story in the following terms: the Prophet Noah stands for the Imamate; the boat and those in it for the community of believers who know the

Imam of the time; and the remainder who perish in the Flood for those who refuse to recognise the Imam.

8.3 The Allegory of Incorporation

I later interviewed the interpreter in the presence of a few learned Ismailis, and informed him that I had heard another interpretation of the same story from an Ismaili elsewhere in Khurasan. He immediately replied: 'Ah, that is the meaning of the story as it applies to the body! Noah stands for the spirit within us, the boat for [the body] that houses the spirit, and the Flood for the lower self (*nafs-i ammāra*) which is within us.'

It is important to note the following points arising from our encounter. First, beneath the narrative there is the *bāṭin*, the allegory that locates the Imam and his true following within the deeper procession of divine grace. Beneath that is another hermeneutic level, the *bāṭin* of the *bāṭin*, the allegory that, in a reflexive manner, 'in-corporates' meaning, transposing events described in religious narrative into events of the soul. Second, the interpreter admitted the other exegesis only after he sensed I was aware of it; additionally, he did not see himself as inconsistent in offering and accepting such widely-differing interpretations. We shall explore this apparent 'inconsistency' of meanings later, because it has profound implications on the nature of religious language and knowledge.

8.4 The Capacity to Entertain Plurality of Meaning

The key and oft-repeated notion is the capacity of this or that individual to understand the nature of things. The Ismailis of Iran refer to this capacity as *ẓarfiyyat*, which comes from the Persian word for bowl.

This is how the issue of ẓarfiyyat was expained to me: One of Prophet Muhammad's associates asked him why there were stars in the sky, and he answered that they were to decorate the heavens. When another man later asked the Prophet the same question, he gave a complex elucidation of the principles of

astronomy. A man who witnessed both incidents was flabber-
gasted. He confronted the Prophet with the stark contrast
between the two explanations, and the Prophet said that the
capacity (ẓarfīyyat) of the first man was such that he was not
able to understand more. To the Ismailis, the importance of
such capacity goes beyond the ability to comprehend things.
There is danger of confusion, misunderstanding or worse when
higher knowledge spills over to those who do not have the capacity for absorbing it. The Iranian Ismailis repeatedly warn
about this peril as in the following lines:

> Zinhār, zinhār, bih zabān nakhwānid, bih qalb bikhwānid,
> bih rūz nakhwānid, bih shab bikhwānid.

> Beware, beware, say it not with your tongue, but with your heart;
> say it not by day, but by night.

In one context, therefore, an Ismaili might readily agree with
the idea of bodily ressurrection (*mu ʿād*), saying that since God
has created us, surely on the Day of Reckoning (*rūz-i qiyāmat*)
He can resurrect us. In another context, however, the same
person might say that resurrection refers in essence to the re-
awakening of the soul upon union with the spirit within, the
rebirth of a person at the extinguishing of the lower self after
sustained meditation on the Names of God.

9. Conclusions: The Plurality of Meaning and the Meaning of Plurality

We have seen in the above discussion the various settings among
the Ismailis in which religious belief finds expression and allows for gradations of meaning. Before we explore the
implications of such gradations for our understanding of the
religious life, some remarks on Islam in rural areas are in order.

9.1 Understanding Rural Mysticism

With regard to religious narrative, the traditional mystics may
have been more subtle and imaginative than their educated

offspring, but they did not think quite as tidily. An old man would recite and explain the most sublime images of Rumi, then with blithe credulity tell of how certain pure-hearted people jumped into burning ovens to emerge unsinged. Another would talk of a spiritual sage who turned into an aged man, then a child, at the blink of an eye. This habit of mixing magic and allegory repelled the urbanised young generation. The ears of the young sophisticates, trained on the importance of modern rational thought, would stop listening; their eyes, aware of the decisive power of controlled experiment, would turn down in frustrated politeness; and later, when the young were with their peers in the alleys, the jokes would fly.

But when we look closer, we see among the youth more than a rejection of the miraculous. Ridicule lives in the shadow of shame from which it tries to escape. Some of the educated, urbanised Ismailis were not a little embarrassed by their parents' thick accents, peasant ways and rude clothing. A book had been published in Iran criticising a whole range of 'superstitions' among the rural people. The emotions of the educated migrants were too close to a past they wished to escape. This prevented a more measured and benign response to the religious imagination of their elders in the rural areas.

Some religious empathy is required to place these narratives of rural folk in the world from which they appeared. These stories are not the wild and woolly concoctions of ignorant and isolated villagers. They are daring re-enactments of imagery with its roots in the Qur'an, and they must be understood as the narrative equivalents of poetic imagery and as examples of the mythic imagination made concrete.

The original story, the fecund image of trial by fire, is that of the Prophet Ibrahim, whom Nimrod had thrown into the fire to see if the God he claimed to worship would save him.[18] As these Ismailis might have said, 'Ibrahim survived his test, and so must we ours, if we claim to have attained the truth and to have found spiritual purity.' For them, to jump into a live fire is an experiment of daring, a trust in the empiricism of burning flesh. This apparent recklessness of faith in the testability of the spirit is quite consistent with their impatience with mere hope for heaven and dread of hell in the afterlife. These practices arise from their desire for the tangibility of the divine.

In a rural society so beholden to nature, such desires are rife. Magical practices abound throughout Khurasan and in rural Iran. Dotting the landscape are a wide range of shrines to which people go to make a vow to sacrifice a sheep if their child survives the grave illness, passes the decisive exam or marries the right person. As has been shown earlier, the soot from cotton wicks burned at the shrine is smeared around the eyes of children to ward off the evil eye. The truth of immanent spirituality must be tangible for it to find a place in the daily trials of life. However, there is yet more to these practices.

Iranian society is ancient, and intermingled with the culture are the reconstituted elements of what are likely to have been pre-Islamic religious traditions. The practice of burning cotton wick throughout the region may well have been among the bargains early Muslim proselytisers made with the adherents of ancient faiths, in this case the Zoroastrian tradition, in order to set deep roots among them. A more obvious example of such accommodation is the festival of Nawruz, the ancient celebration of the Persian new year on the vernal equinox.

Let us return to the repulsion of the educated generation by the magical beliefs and practices prevalent in the rural areas. This feeling reflects a far more general prejudice, deeper and more insidious. It is the prejudice of the urban, educated elite against rural and popular expressions of religion. As Mohammed Arkoun puts it, at the root of the prejudice is the dominion of the written over the oral, the formal over the informal, 'orthodoxy' over 'heterodoxy', and the desire to narrow authority over interpretation.[19] These categories, so often used in modern scholarship within and beyond the social sciences, are useful only to a point. These dichotomies are not hard and fast: within every community there are those who are closer to the text than to the oral. There are some who have more prestige on account of their learning and others who live on the fringes of common belief. What is crucial is a fuller understanding of the orality of faith and a greater respect for its place in a religious community and in the history of the faith.

What is behind these crippling prejudices? In academic circles, although there is growing awareness of 'popular religion' among experts on Islam, the interest is too often tinged with patronising curiosity. According to them, peasants demonstrate not Islam, but 'islam', which is little more than Islam distorted quaintly by ignorance and isolation. For them, the 'real' Islam exists in texts and learned discourse. This Islam is the conception enshrined by many great Orientalists in an on-going rapport with urban holders of the tradition who, in their anxiety to shake off the fetters of ignorance and backwardness, claim sole authority to interpret the faith. For both the Orientalist and the urban Muslim legist, the lived understanding of great poetry and doctrines expounded by rural folk are no more than a text roughly approximated, mere shreds scattered at random among ill-informed and uncritical peasants, a record of which can at best produce no more than a distorted and distant echo of the pristine truth of the text. The learned peasant is a poor and embarrassing relation who has suddenly moved into the house of the scholar with scant thought to the latter's dignity.

A number of anthropologists have examined and championed the place of popular religion, and are to be credited with giving due attention to rural thought and to positioning religious debate in the context of social movements. Others have with superb skill linked the study of a textual tradition with practices of popular religion. But all too many have left rural populations in isolation from the history of traditions, treating them as interesting examples of provincial syncretism. Thus, in their reckoning, there is a great tradition and many little traditions, there is the centre and the periphery, there is the formal and the informal. In these excisions from intellectual history, such distinctions do a disservice to the imaginative life that individuals can lend to the text. It is here that the rural Ismaili mystics really stand out, not in the abstract sophistication of their doctrine but in the subtle shades of meaning that lend life to the poetic texts they have in their possession.

9.2 Man, Nature and Instrumental Religion

Whatever the general prejudices of urban against rural dwellers, the superstitions and magical practices of the latter have found critics from within, as the following remarks about a smaller shrine elsewhere in Khurasan reveal:

> I used to go to the shrine of Qadam-gah ... it is near someone's field that has, as a result, acquired *barakat* (grace). He planted melons but they were all worm-eaten. The *barakat* was obviously meant only for the worms! I noticed a mouse scamper out from under one of the stones at the shrine and disappear under another, and said to myself 'Ay, is this the pilgrimage-site where Hazrat 'Abbas or Hazrat 'Ali came and left an imprint of his foot?'... Several years ago [a number of villagers, including some learned Ismailis] went and set fire to a shrine at the spring nearby. When they got back, everybody said that the whole village would suffer. Yet what a year we had – lots of rain and a good crop of wheat!

These critiques raise disturbing questions from the very premises of the mystical tradition. As we have seen, the greatest insights of the rural mystics were to find within the events of the Qur'an fecund and morally resonant images. Such images can direct the yearning soul toward the riches within the heart in the midst of life rather than toward the mere promise of heaven in the life after death. Why reduce an event of the souls of men, whose mission and whose poetry was to awaken humanity to a deeper, less literal faith, to the crass materiality of the evil eye or miracles in hot ovens?

In its relationship with nature, humanity must balance dangerous dependency and destructive exploitation. The peasant or farmer can least escape the paradox that has haunted the human race since the dawn of agriculture. He or she will propitiate and bargain with fickle nature at every turn of the yearly cycle. Religion cannot but be involved here. In this matter the mystic impulse should be wary if it is to transcend the rural world in which it struck such deep roots. To regain its universal appeal, mysticism should aim to expunge contractual elements in our relationship to nature. Here, as early social theorists such as Saint Simon pointed out, science must replace magic, public health reduce the fear of wanton death, good education strengthen the link between ability and success, and sound economic and social policies give peasants greater control over their destiny. And for the mystic, instrumental religion must here make way for the mythic and the metaphysical foundations of respect for the natural order. An importance source of inspiration for such a relationship with nature is in the Qur'an:[20]

> And of His Signs
> is your slumbering by night and day
> and your seeking after His bounty.
> Surely in that are Sins for people who hear.
> And of His Signs
> He shows you lightning, for fear and hope,
> and that He sends down out of heaven water,
> and He revives the earth after it is dead.

Such an attitude to the natural order is far from the strident voice of those who decry the way industrial society has defaced nature in the name of progress. A firm but quieter sensibility is needed, a voice that keeps in mind this covenant with God and His creation, as well as the fate of all future generations, that coolly measures the benefit obtained today against the price which later generations may have to pay. Once shorn of the elements of instrumental religion, the pilgrimages can still retain their mysterious power to evoke such truths. Through their rich endowment of myths and rituals, they can consecrate the complex bond between man and nature on the one hand, and man and his past on the other hand.

9.3 Allegory and the Reflexive Imagination

Allegory, is more formulaic than other tropes such as metaphor. It poses a fixed destination and sets a lower limit to the imagination than metaphor. Moreover, since it is formulaic, it can suffer the fate of all formulae: it can become standardised and can consequently be applied unthinkingly. Furthermore, because it sets few bounds on its application, allegory can be applied rampantly. However, a broader perspective is required than to see allegory simply as a hobbled relative of metaphor. The importance of the *bāṭin*, the intrinsic signification of things, among the Ismailis highlights the dangers posed by singularity of meaning; it provides an intelligible and efficient weapon against the tyranny of the literal. Allegory preserved the religious imagination of the Ismailis through centuries of persecution and danger.

This rite of imagination lies at the heart of Iranian Ismailism. The precautionary caution of the Ismailis, their carefully-guarded boundaries, as well as what appeared to others as their elitism, emerged partly because of the intolerance of their neighbours from which they suffered for many centuries. Most interestingly, three features of crucial importance allowed these Iranian mystics to embrace the momentum of history:

(i) Allegory turned history into a metaphor for the inner life, allowing the Iranian Ismailis to distinguish between form and essence, to inject movement into history, even to see change in form as sometimes necessary to preserve the essence. Allegory enabled them to accommodate the vast changes demanded by the modern world on their own terms.

(ii) However formulaic, allegory enabled the Ismailis to go beyond the literal, thus giving prime position to personal interpretation. Esoteric doctrine thrives when it is protected by the barriers of the oral tradition, in lively conversation, competing interpretation and reflection. It suffers in a world of slogans and uniformity of belief. The esoteric must have one feature if it is to survive in fact rather in name: it may be susceptible to interpretations that differ markedly, but these interpretations must cohabit in peace.

(iii) Allegory can powerfully encourage the imagination to be reflexive, enabling religious narrative to turn into a mirror for personal ethics. For the Ismailis, this process shifted the debates on ritual practices from the question of conformity to the ethical and spiritual signification of these practices.

We now turn to the wider significance of this issue.

9.4 Between Dogma and Total Freedom

The Ismailis of Iran have a clear idea of the basic principles of the faith, that is, belief in the Oneness (*tawḥīd*) of God, in the Prophet Muhammad, in a living Imam as the guide of the believers, etc. But they all maintain that people differ from one another in their capacity, and that the difference in personal capacity must be respected in the plurality of religious belief. Hence, there is the view among them that, beyond the few fundamentals of the faith, there is no single entity called Ismaili doctrine. It cannot mean one and the same thing to everybody. In all their discussions on allegorical interpretation, nowhere among these people did I find a hint of compulsion, that is to say, the belief that to be an Ismaili, one must take this or that to be the exclusive, received meaning of a text. This perspective explains their disdain for all forms of literalism and blind imitation (*taqlīd*) in religious matters, even though they may not have been consistent in this belief.

This respect for diversity, however, does not imply intellectual or spiritual equality in the status of individuals. The Ismailis believe that, in view of the varying human capacities to understand the complexities of interpretation, there is an elite. But the ranks of this elite are not in any sense determined by wealth or formal education, or by any other ascriptive criteria such as heredity, age, race or gender. It is simply the product of the different temperaments of human beings, the possibilities for which emerged on that first day that Adam's body was created from the four elements. Similarly, they all share the assumption, implicitly and unequivocally, that the *bāṭin* is of a higher order and reflects a greater depth of understanding than the *ẓāhir*.

The history of Europe and elsewhere has shown the appalling cruelties inflicted by institutions that attempted to enforce a uniform dogma, particularly through the machinery of state power. Modern nation states have often found the promotion of dogma a useful instrument of power, in the same way as religious authority tends to determine itself by virtue of obedience to standard tenets or practices. Modern participatory democracies in the West have, after centuries, evolved and institutionalised principles of freedom of belief and of the separation of church and state. Simultaneously, in a variety of faiths, attempts are being made to counteract the total abandonment of religious principles in the public arena by dragging one or another aspect of their dogmas into the arena of politics. The issue tends to polarise between the total abandonment of fundamental ethical direction on the one hand and the enforcement of dogmatic principles on the other, a dilemma that has recently been recounted in a lucid and moving novel.[21]

The assumption behind the polarised notion of dogma is that because religion proposes a metaphysical foundation for its principles, because religion must further enact them in society, and finally, because a community of believers is maintained by conformity to such principles, the inevitable result is standardisation and the enforcement of dogma.

The case being made here is that this is only partially true: religion does imply dogma, but not its rigid imposition on everybody regardless of individual propensities and capacities. Allegory offers one viable compromise between a profound contradiction in religious knowledge and its institutionalisation. This is the conflict between the need to resonate with individual conscience, which calls for diversity in interpretation, and the need to maintain a community of believers, which calls for conformity to the common denominator. The Ismailis of Iran have given a vital and important place to diversity without compromising their sense of identity as a community. They have shown one path a person of faith can take between rock-hard dogma and the utter fluidity of freedom.

9.5 Context as a Sanctuary for the Plurality of Meaning

This essay illustrates how the diversity of interpretation of the Qur'an and of devotional poetry reposes, or finds sanctuary, in the oral context. This raises a much larger issue, namely the role of oral context in contemporary life.

We live in a paradoxical age. In the realm of scholarship, the text is supreme, while in the public realm, television is ubiquitous. Both features of the intellectual landscape conspire to reduce the importance of context. In this connection, Joshua Meyerovitz has broken new ground in his study of the implications of television for society.[22] Instead of focusing only on the content, he examines television as a medium, and takes his analysis well beyond that of Marshall McLuhan. His basic point is that, unlike television, a book which has to be obtained by individual purchase or borrowing is not accessible to everyone at any one time. Moreover, the privacy offered by the closed door protects parents from exposing their conflicts and concerns to their children. There are rules for access to the book (literacy, technical proficiency, age), and until recently in Western society at least, there have been rules that determined discourse in various contexts.

Television, on the other hand, has broken all the bounds of context. This is because, through investigative reporting and situation comedies, television shows the 'off-stage' behaviour of politicians and public figures, as well as that of parents, whose errors, concerns and private discussions are presented not only to any member of the family who can switch the machine on, but also to the entire family sitting together in one room. This phenomenon, suggests Meyerovitz, has exercised profound social and psychological effects. In American political life, one notes a greater concern with visual criteria such as appearance and ease of manner rather than with intellectual criteria in the judgment of politicians. In family life, the breaking of the bounds of context has resulted in a decrease in the authority of parents over children. In ordinary discourse, this trend has blurred distinctions between formal and informal speech. Finally, a blurring has taken place in the way males and females dress or cross-dress. What is of particular interest here is the suggestion that the appreciation of context is disappearing in modern society. More and more, things are expected to be the same to everybody. Plurality is primarily in the choice offered by numerous TV channels.

Over the last few decades there also appears to have been a resurgence of religious movements that insist upon single and literal truth of the religious text as the unchanging core of the faith. Debates about the creation of the world as described in the Bible hinge on the scientific validity of the age of the earth or of the universe; debates about the creation of man hinge on whether Darwin or the Bible is right. The spread of printed media, on the other hand, has increased the perception that what is written is more important and more permanent than what is oral. What has retreated from the general arena of religious belief are the notions that a religious text can have layers of meaning that coexist with their respective standards of validity, that religious narrative can be understood through literary analysis and can be appreciated for the power of the image without losing its link with the divine.

The extraordinary power of the text lies in the simple fact that it can survive context, that is, it can outlast the time and place of the verbal utterance. Moreover, it turns the act of reading into a special, personal event, which allows for a unique and flexible encounter between the author who creates a world and the reader who enters it – as anyone who has sat in an armchair with a good book can confirm. Finally, a text can fix and enforce reality. All three features of the text are particularly important for the preservation and development of culture.

The fact that the text can survive the verbal utterance means that it can widen intellectual discourse and, more generally, it can perpetuate civilisation long after its living bearers have disappeared. Perhaps the single greatest defining moment of a civilisation is the appearance of writing. For instance, it is difficult to exaggerate the importance to Islamic civilisation of the moment when al-Farabi chanced upon an Arabic translation of Aristotle in a bookshop. That started such an opening of the mind, such a centuries-long conversation, such a quickening of culture! This episode makes one ponder how fragile is the text: it is on paper so thin, so tearable, so burnable, so susceptible to the corrosion of time and the elements. The medieval city of Baghdad was renowned for its cultural splendours under the Abbasids; yet so little remains of it that scholars today are unsure of its configuration. But the ideas, the poetry, the philosophy that its citizens produced in its days of glory, have survived the centuries of the rise and fall of cities and empires to come down to us on mere sheets of paper.

The text inscribes reality in several ways. A novel creates a world that you, as a reader, can enter. Moreover, this fictional world, upon entry, becomes your world; and if the novel is a great one, like all great works of art it will push open the boundaries of your world and force you, for example, to see life differently, or to understand human motivation better. For evidence of the immense potential of the text one need only look at the lengths to which authoritarian regimes will go to punish independent-minded writers. A Russian once said that if a hundred years from now the question is asked, 'Who was Brezhnev?' the answer will be, 'He was someone who lived in the time of Solzhenitsyn.'

In the realm of daily action, the text can also enforce reality, especially where the rule of law prevails. No lawyer or businessman needs reminding of the value of the phrase, 'Get it in writing!'

Context is more difficult to define. To put it most simply, context is what is said to whom within a particular boundary. This boundary is usually physical space, such as a room in which people can talk in privacy. Context can also be invisible, such as a language shared only by some of the people present or, more subtly, words, hints or gestures understood by only a few. The most crucial feature of context is that it is created by a boundary of some sort. A text is an object, whereas a context is a situation. A text is fixed once it is inscribed, while context is fluid. Control over a text is ultimately limited because it can be disseminated and distributed almost indefinitely. Control over a context is by definition much more effective. Text works by dissemination, while context works by closure. Context tends to form boundaries of groups, whereas text tends toward informing everybody.

An essential complement to the poetic and historical texts of a community is lived understanding, for it is the latter which awakens meaning. Mystical thought and discourse can only be understood properly in the orality that surrounds and protects the layers of meaning that a great poetic text renders possible. It is essential to preserve such a plurality of meaning because it befits the diversity of human beings and offers the gradations of insight that are vital steps in the journey towards God.

9.6 Towards a Pluralistic Notion of Muslim Civilisation

The argument for a plurality of meaning goes much further than its role in the vitality of mystical thought. It speaks to the very idea of Islam that we entertain. To speak of there being one single set of ideas or system of thought called 'Islamic', or 'Ismaili' for that matter, is a monolithic fantasy that pervades much of current thinking on Islam as a phenomenon.

To encompass a plurality of meaning within Islam means we must reconsider the concept of diversity in Muslim societies. Diversity in Islam is not some essence that has been contaminated by local differences or foreign influences. Muslims from the very beginning have been in constant and creative interaction with local traditions and regional cultures. Diversity is therefore a measure of breadth and tolerance rather than a problem that calls for explanation or a return to the centre. But respect for diversity, however important as a starting point, cannot serve as the sole objective of religious thought.

The Muslims of today have barely begun the major task of grappling with the vast social, technical and intellectual transformation that has gripped the world in the last three centuries. The mystical, the legal and the rational-intellectual each have a role to play in this task, each with its strengths, each reliant on the others to compensate for its weaknesses. The legal-minded dimension in Islam is required to the extent that the law helps provide some parameters for the religious community and a foundation for norms of justice and fairness within the various Muslim communities. However, the rational and legal domains cannot satisfy the soul searching for the truth behind the promise of the Qur'an, that having come from God, so we shall return.[23]

Neither of these two domains can attend to the need for freedom in individual interpretation, or offer the succour of divine love that the great poets have spoken of with such inspired longing. But the mystic, in his suspicion of everyday rationality, if unrestrained, can have a corrosive effect on human advancement in knowledge and technology which rests on a commitment to rational and empirical tools of inquiry. The rush for mystical certainty can short-circuit the task of individuals, as much as of a civilisation, to cope with a changing world. On the other hand, when the mystic points to the divine as the source of knowledge, we should be in awe of the intuition that is the fountainhead of creative thought, be it in the mathematical equations of Albert Einstein or in the fertile imagery of Jalal al-Din Rumi. The example of the mystic can inspire us to bow our heads in humility whenever we approach such boundaries of human reason.

Notes

1. For an excellent survey of Ismaili history, see Farhad Daftary, *The Ismāʿīlīs: Their History and Doctrines* (Cambridge: Cambridge University Press, 1990).

2. The focus here is on pilgrimages among the Ismailis who give unique meaning to them, but such pilgrimages are, of course, a common feature of popular Shiʿi piety in Iran. As a matter of fact, the villages referred to in this section are not exclusively Ismaili, and Twelver Shiʿis also participate significantly in such pilgrimages.

3. This event is figurative of that in the Qur'an (7:107) when Moses proves his spiritual mettle against the Pharaoh.

4. The story has several versions which differ in detail from one another.

5.   A similar phenomenon appears to have taken place in Soviet Central Asia, where visits to tombs of Sufi saints and political martyrs became focal points of popular dissent in the face of totalitarian suffocation.

6.   Victor Turner's *Structure and Antistructure* (Chicago: Aldine, 1969) is a valuable source of insight on this matter.

7.   R. H. Keshavjee, 'The Power of Games and the Games of Power in Rural Iran,' *Iranian Studies*, 22 (1989), pp. 87–97.

8.   This idea corresponds closely to lines of Omar Khayyam which are commonly known in Iran: *Dūzakh sharari-yi z-ranj-i bīhūda-i māst; Firdaws damī-yi z-vaqt-i āsūda-yi māst* (Hell is the agony of our futile pain; Paradise is a taste of the fleeting moment of our bliss). Shahla Haeri, personal communication.

9.   The reference here is to the *ḥadīth qudsī*, 'Heaven and the earth contain Me not, but the heart of the faithful servant contains Me,' cited by Annemarie Schimmel, *Mystical Dimensions of Islam* (Chapel Hill: University of North Carolina Press, 1975), p. 190, from Badiʿ al-Zaman Furuzanfar's *Aḥādith-i Mathnawī* (Tehran, 1334 sh./1955).

10.   The crisis of culture that emerges when instrumental objectives cannot be rooted in some shared philosophical basis is eloquently conveyed about American culture by Robert Bellah et al. in *Habits of the Heart* (Berkeley: University of California Press, 1985).

11.   Note that in this question the Persian term *insān* is not linked to gender.

12.   The Persian puns the word for self (*khud*) and God (*khudā*).

13.   Ref. Qur'an, 5:3.

14.   Ref. Qur'an, 89:27–28.

15.   Persian language styles are finely nuanced by context. There is a variation in style approporiate to various contexts of intimacy and hierarchy. A rough and residual equivalent of this can be seen in the *tu-vous* distinction in French.

16.   Ref. Qur'an, 7:59–64, 11:25–49, 23:23–30, 26:105–122, 29:14–16, 71:1–28.

17.   The word 'myth' has unfortunately acquired a common pejorative sense as something that is fictitious or purely imaginary. The vitality of myth does not lie in its verisimilitude but in its capacity to suggest meanings beneath overt events. The meaning employed here is from anthropology, where the mythic is a vital link in the chain of meanings that connect ritual action with ideas and elements of society.

18.   Ref. Qur'an, 21: 51–71.

19.   Mohammed Arkoun, personal communication.

20.   Qur'an, 30:23–24.

21. Jill Paton Walsh, *Knowledge of Angels* (Cambridge, UK: Green Bay Press, 1994).

22. Joshua Meyerowitz, *No Sense of Place* (Oxford: Oxford University Press, 1985).

23. Ref. Qur'an, 2:156.